Table of Contents

Preface

In other books in this series, we've discussed how groups work and how to make them more effective. We've presented principles and practices that develop strong, productive groups, and maintain their well-being. This book discusses and describes methods and techniques to understand what's going on in the group, what the potential of various members is, and which individuals are having a good or bad experience.

Methods for identifying critical points within the larger organization and within other groups are also discussed because groups are situated in a context that also needs to be understood for a group to function effectively. This book focuses on assessing group dynamics and group development from both an internal and external perspective.

For an established group to function effectively, members must agree on its purpose, activities, goals, procedures, and preferred beliefs. The group's rules, policies, and norms represent proper behaviour. When a group's standards are well-accepted by members, each person knows how to act, what to anticipate from colleagues, and how the member and the group members can work together smoothly. In a group with high cohesiveness, members want the group to succeed so that it can continue to provide the satisfaction that initially made the group attractive to them. Members must have regularly supplied information about how well their group is performing and be able to compare these scores over time.

As workers with groups in business settings, organizational units, educational delivery, and social service contexts, we use groups to help individuals achieve desired organizational, personal, and interpersonal goals. As workers with groups, we also want to increase individual and group performance and productivity. To accomplish these goals, we have to understand the groups we work with and gain practical knowledge in order to plan strategies to assist groups in greater effectiveness and productivity.

To understand any group, we need methods and tools for undertaking an assessment or conducting research. Methods are the tools — the instruments, techniques, and procedures by which we can gain and interpret information about the groups we are facilitating and managing. Different methods can achieve different things and have certain advantages as well as some limitations. This book highlights some tools that give the study of groups a foothold in the scientific tradition and provide credible reports of a group's well-being and achievements.

Hedley G. Dimock
Irene Devine
December, 1996

PART ONE	Collecting Group Information

"It's surprising how much you can find out by asking."

Leaders who can diagnose the climate and dynamics of their groups can make more useful interventions and guide their groups more successfully toward the achievement of their goals. There are three functions of assessing a group:

1. to find out what is happening.
2. to figure out or diagnose why it is happening.
3. to anticipate future directions for the group.

As with visiting your medical doctor, it's helpful to be assessed before you are 'sick' to provide a basis for comparison and some perspective on the sickness. Regular assessments chart weight, blood pressure, temperature, and general functioning. When problems arise, this information is recharted in an attempt to diagnose the problem.

Groups function in an environment. Specifically, most groups operate as part of an organization, they interact with other groups, are part of a community and external system or society. The norms, values, and activities of a group — its usual ways of doing things — are very much influenced by these external forces. A full understanding of a group requires an assessment of these external influences as well as the internal dynamics of the group.

The third purpose of group assessment is less common as it's an anticipatory diagnosis. It's a proactive assessment of future trends to identify new objectives for the group and prepare the group to utilize new kinds of resources.

Direct observation is the most frequently used and likely the most important method of gathering information about a group. Yet, assessments by the members are more accurate and reliable and can be quite exciting to use. These methods include needs assessment and interest locators, group reports and diaries, member descriptions and nominations, reputation ratings, and surveys of the group, organization, and community. Group members usually feel these assessments are more credible than observations which tend to be lopsided in reflecting the observer's priorities and interests. Our approach is to always try to combine data collection methods

1

regarding important issues and to triangulate the information, that is, confirm the data using three different approaches.

When it comes to knowing what's going on in a group or what the potential of various members is, the group as a whole knows more than the supervisor/manager. Thus, cadets in training are more able to predict future leaders than their staff officers, students can identify problem students more accurately than their teachers, and workers can guess who is going to quit much better than their managers. Self-description and reports or nominations by others provide remarkable insights about a group. Their accuracy and credibility encourage their frequent use to assess the developmental level and stage of growth of a group. Regular surveys of the work group by the members also provide feedback for group empowerment and performance. Peer coaching in self-help and training groups is steadily increasing as is peer review for performance appraisal. By the turn of the century, performance appraisals by peers will likely be as common as the traditional appraisal by the supervisor. Peer appraisal in the classroom is also on the rise, specifically for group projects where students work together to produce one product.

Observational Methods

Other books in this series discuss observation as an effective method in collecting information that can be used to assist a group in becoming more productive. For example, Part Two of *How to Observe Your Group*, discusses observation guides and developmental areas that can be observed. *Managing Dynamic Groups*, discusses observer reports and process evaluation sessions as techniques to collect data from a group that can then be used in replanning for effectiveness. There are various approaches to observation but the goal of any observational measure is always the same; to watch and record events that transpire in groups in order to understand the group's dynamics. We will briefly review observations as a method of assessing groups.

Participant Observation

We can study a group from within by actually being a member of the group. This technique is called participant observation in so much that the observer is in a face-to-face relationship with the group members and participates with them in their natural setting.

Covert Observation

When we study a group from within we may indirectly influence the group's behaviour. There's a tendency for people to modify behaviour when they know they're being observed. Some people use covert observation, where the observer records the group's activities without the group's knowledge. Although this method may be commendable from a research standpoint, the invasion of privacy is questionable. The use of open, non-deceptive methods is what we advocate and is generally considered to be more ethical and less controversial.

Systematic Structured Observations

Some people collect extensive notes and then try to integrate them to form an overall picture of the group. It's possible to count various observed behaviours according to preestablished classifications. These could include 'number and time' of each member's contributions to the nature of their contributions (task, interpersonal, informative, and so on). Some categories may border on evaluation, but the emphasis is on frequency data that can be analyzed and evaluated at a later point. With the use of videotapes and frequent replays, observations can become very detailed: nonverbals, interruptions, etc. can be easily collected for use at another time.

Observers must learn to identify the types of behaviour in the classification and must practice listening to a group discussion and then breaking the verbal content down into the smallest meaningful unit that can be identified, and then classifying these units as to category. So, considerable training is involved in this form of observation.

Consultant Observers

A guest 'expert' or member of the group may critique a group's efforts in terms of interaction, decision-making methods, and their quality, etc.

A task specialist may be invited from another part of the organization such as human resources, marketing, public relations, or accounting for example, for a fresh view on the group's functioning.

Process Observers

This approach involves helping group members develop insight into the nature of their group's processes. Observers can observe the process of a group by taking note of patterns of communication, decision-making procedures, sources of power, informal social norms, and varieties of inter-member conflict, etc. There are many checklists that can be used, e.g. Likert's Management Diagnosis Chart (1967) or a checklist like the one following, of questions that are relevant to the group.

• Are there clear and accepted group goals?
• Do members seem to be adequately prepared with information?

- Has some procedure, or agenda for the discussion been provided or developed by the group? If so, how well is this being followed? Does it serve the group's needs?
- In a problem-solving discussion, has the group defined and clarified the problem thoroughly, or has it become solution-centred too soon?
- Has judgment been deferred until solutions have been listed and understood by all members?
- When evaluating ideas and opinions, is the group making use of the information brought out during earlier discussion?
- How are decisions being made?
- If needed, has the group made adequate plans to implement its decisions, including member responsibilities, future meetings, and so forth?
- Are special procedural techniques such as brainstorming or parliamentary procedures being used in ways that are productive? Could procedural changes benefit the group?

Once the process observer understands how the group is working, the observations can be discussed with the group and the group members and the process observer can develop ways to improve the group's dynamics.

Communication Networks

The exchange of information among members of a group often follows a stable, predictable pattern. A group's communication network tends to parallel role, status, and attraction patterns and has a powerful impact on group performance and effectiveness and on members' level of satisfaction. A group's communication network influences a variety of group and individual outcomes, including performance.

Video tapes provide rich reminders of the dynamic nature of groups. They can be used for a variety of reasons but certainly, tapes of group interaction are easy to collect, and although analysis is time consuming, they do capture and depict ongoing social interaction and present opportunities to examine dynamics within the group.

Peer Nominations and Sociograms

Self-Report Measures

As the designated leader or manager/supervisor of a group, we want to know how group members feel about something or why they displayed a particular behaviour. A simple solution in finding out what we want to know is to ask questions and record responses. How we go about asking can vary; we can administer carefully constructed questionnaires, distribute attitude surveys, or conduct face-to-face interviews. All these self-report measures are alike in that they involve asking a question and recording the answer.

Self-report measures, (questionnaires, interviews, rating scales), are a direct way, and sometimes the only apparent way, to gain information about certain variables; attitudes, feelings, retrospective recall, and the like. Self-report measures have some serious flaws, for example, respondents may try to answer in some socially desirable way to please the person collecting the information.

Sociometry

Sociometry is an example of a self-report measure. It is a technique for measuring the social relationships linking group members. This technique can be used to summarize graphically and mathematically the patterns of interpersonal attraction in groups. A sociometric study begins by asking group members one or more questions about their fellow members. Typically, the central question concerns which person in the group they like the most, but other questions can be used, such as "Whom in the group would you like to work with the most?" or "Whom do you like the least?"

The place to start in assessing and diagnosing a group is the relationships of the group members. A picture of the *inclusion* of the members is essential. "Who is in and who is out?" or more specifically, "What is the inclusion level of each member?". We want to establish how well each person is accepted by the other members, and how much each person wants to be in the group. Assessing inclusion and acceptance also establishes the relationships among and between members — who is pairing with whom and where the sub-groups or cliques are. How individuals act in a group is influenced by the values and standards that the group sets, and the more an individual is included, the greater this influence will be. Included members seeking recognition in a group will behave rather differently than a fringe member just trying to get included, (see *Making Workgroups Effective*, for more of this dynamic). The inclusion level or social status of group members is best established through a group nomination technique.

In its simplest form, a nomination technique would be a group activity. The number of times a person is nominated shows that person's social status — often called a sociometric position — in the group. Noting the reciprocal choices, (two people who nominate each other), helps to identify pairs and sub-groups which in turn determine the integration or cohesion of the group. Peer nominations are usually charted on a graphic display which is called a **sociogram**. A quick glance at a group's sociogram shows the extent of sub-groups, connections, or cleavages among members, and the overall togetherness of the members. The sociogram also shows the acceptance or inclusion of members and can be used to establish the group's status hierarchy.

Peer nominations can also be used to form new groups or project groups as described in *Making Workgroups Effective* and in *Managing Dynamic Groups*. These may be a task force of a work group, a committee of a board, a classroom group, or the steering committee of an inter-group project. Team building activities within a work group usually involve peer descriptions as a way of helping members think about the group's dynamics and their personal role and function within the group, (see, for example, the **Dimock-Scott Interpersonal Skills Questionnaire** in Figure 1). Sociograms are also helpful in identifying members with problems who may need special assistance.

How to Collect Sociometric Choices

The first task is to decide what you want the nominations to illustrate. Do you want to assess inclusion or acceptance, power, political connections, leadership, influence, or competence in some area? The nomination technique is most meaningful if the question(s) being asked have a practical application that is going to be implemented. This could be a team leader for a project group, classmates for a case study team, car companions for a national conference, membership for a board committee, or shift mates of a patient care team.

Often, the questions asked elicit a different response, as the person you'd choose to facilitate the meeting, if the chairperson were absent, may be different from whom you'd nominate to be your representative on an inter-group council, or who you'd choose as a car companion for a long trip. The chairperson may have competence in facilitating short purposeful meetings; the representative may be affable and persuasive; while the trip companion may be a person you like or want to get to know the most. Hence, it may make sense to ask all three questions, then chart and compare the responses. Each nomination chart or sociogram should show the criteria used as the basis for selection.

If, as we have suggested, the results are going to be used to form groups for the specified activities, the implementation person or team now needs to follow through and do the best job possible to arrange the groups on the basis of choices. This is easier said than done as some members are usually underchosen or left out. Our solution has been to place these members with one of the people they choose. This means that some groups will include a person they chose last or not at all. We feel this is more likely to promote their acceptance and integration than to group all of the unchosen people

FIGURE 1

Interpersonal Skills Questionnaire

by Hedley Dimock and Doug Scott

This questionnaire is to be used in describing a work colleague or associate. Circle the response which best describes how this person tends to behave.

	1 Rarely	2 Sometimes	3 Often	4 Most of time	5 Almost always
1. This person is clear in describing his/her preferences and expectations for me and others.	1	2	3	4	5
2. This person is prepared to listen attentively to me when I am expressing my thoughts and feelings.	1	2	3	4	5
3. I can trust this person with my private ideas and opinions.	1	2	3	4	5
4. This person is sensitive and aware of how I am feeling in our mutual activities.	1	2	3	4	5
5. This person is open and flexible in implementing new ideas and proposals of others.	1	2	3	4	5
6. This person helps me feel included and supported in the group.	1	2	3	4	5
7. This person is open to receiving feedback on his/her behaviour and its impact on me.	1	2	3	4	5
8. Personal concerns and problems of this person related to work are disclosed to me.	1	2	3	4	5
9. It is quite easy for me to have a talk with this person whenever I have the desire or need.	1	2	3	4	5
10. When I go to this person with a problem about my work, I know I'll get thoughtful criticism and constructive help.	1	2	3	4	5
11. This person's manner makes it easy for me to tell him/her when things aren't going as well as expected.	1	2	3	4	5
12. This person gives me commendation and recognition for a job well done.	1	2	3	4	5
13. This person is ready to confront me and others and deal with any possible conflicts.	1	2	3	4	5
14. When we are discussing group problems, this person asks for my ideas and opinions.	1	2	3	4	5

together. The rationale is that the other members of the highly chosen groups are the most able, through their inclusion and security, to provide energy for the integration of the underchosen.

There is no definite number of nominations that should be asked for, and research on this point varies a great deal. The rule of thumb in our studies has been to ask for three choices if the group is less than 15 in number, and to ask for five choices if it is over 15. If the question asks the member to nominate people from inside and outside the group, ten choices may be asked for. This has worked out quite well as long as the participants are at least 11 years old.

One of the variables that should be considered in large groups where members make their choices in the presence of another, is the physical presence of all the group members at that time. Everyone, especially teenagers and adolescents, tend to leave the absent members out of their nominations. In adult groups we remind the members of who is missing and with youth groups we list their names on a flipchart or chalkboard. When members of a large group make their nomination away from the group, we give them a written list of all the names to provide the virtual visibility of everyone.

Figure 2 shows three samples of nomination questions.

FIGURE 2   *Sample Nominating Questions*

In August, most of us will be attending the national convention held this year in Niagara Falls. In order to help arrange transportation, please list the three people with whom you would like to ride. While you won't get exactly who you choose, it will assist us in doing a better job of assigning seats.

My first choice is _____
My second choice is _____
My third choice is _____

(Nominations based on friendship)

* * * *

Think back over the last few meetings of the Board of Directors and some of the decisions we have made. Then, list below three people who have most frequently influenced your thinking.

The three people are:

_____, _____, _____

(Nominations based on influence)

* * * *

...continued

If we were planning to introduce a special project into our group, (organization), who are the three people you would suggest to have on the steering committee to ensure the project gets off to a good start?

1. _____
2. _____
3. _____

(Nominations based on political competence)

How to Construct a Sociogram

After the nominations have been collected from all the group members, a chart is prepared to tabulate and diagram the choices. Figure 4 was designed for small groups of not more than eight members. Figures 5 and 6 are for larger groups. The choices of two members of our sample group, the Anzacks, (a pre-teen group at a local 'Y') are used in Figure 3 to illustrate how the information is put on the chart.

Friendship patterns in a group often become more clear if, in completing the diagram in the lower half of the page, the first

---

FIGURE 3   *Sample Anzacks Questions for Friendship Chart*

Your name: *Grant Ruple* _____

List below the three people in our group you would most like to share sleeping quarters with on our next night out.

First choice: *Bob King* _____
Second choice: *Tom Smith* _____
Third choice: *Joe Bryant* _____

* * * *

Your name: *Bob King* _____

List below the three people in our group you would most like to share sleeping quarters with on our next night out.

First choice: *Phil Donald* _____
Second choice: *Tom Smith* _____
Third choice: *Grant Ruple* _____

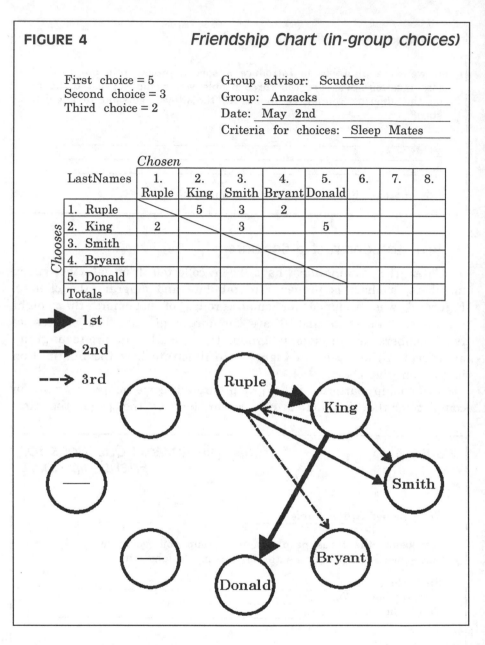

FIGURE 4 *Friendship Chart (in-group choices)*

First choice = 5
Second choice = 3
Third choice = 2

Group advisor: Scudder
Group: Anzacks
Date: May 2nd
Criteria for choices: Sleep Mates

Chosen

Chooses LastNames	1. Ruple	2. King	3. Smith	4. Bryant	5. Donald	6.	7.	8.
1. Ruple		5	3	2				
2. King	2		3		5			
3. Smith								
4. Bryant								
5. Donald								
Totals								

➤ 1st
→ 2nd
--→ 3rd

choices of everyone are put in first, then all the second choices, and finally the third. Between each round, the group worker can pause and get a picture of the group at a different level. Some boys receive no first choices but several second choices and this is highlighted in the three-step process.

For a larger group, the chart in the upper half of Figure 4 can be expanded and five choices can be shown. Figure 5 is set up in this way.

FIGURE 5   *Another Friendship Chart*
                                                 (in-group choices)

Date _____ Worker _____

Criteria for choices _____ Choices Group _____

Weight for 3 choices   Weight for 5 choices
  1st = 5   1st = 9   4th = 4
  2nd = 3   2nd = 7   5th = 3
  3rd = 2   3rd = 5

Chosen

Choosers

Total

No. of 1st
choices

No. of 2nd
choices

No. of 3rd
choices

No. of
choosers
who are
also chosen

11

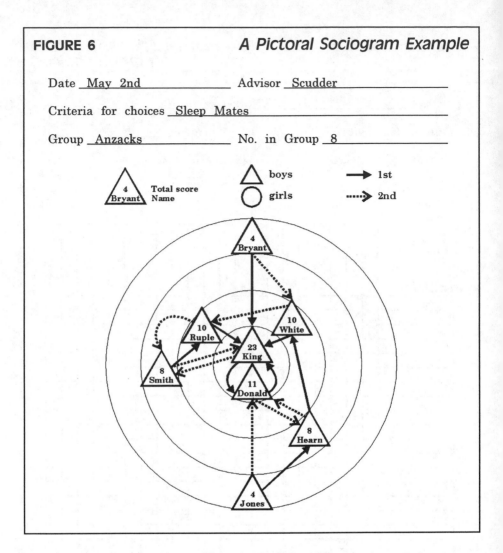

FIGURE 6 — *A Pictoral Sociogram Example*

Date _May 2nd_ Advisor _Scudder_

Criteria for choices _Sleep Mates_

Group _Anzacks_ No. in Group _8_

Total score / Name

boys — △   girls — ○

1st ——→   2nd ·····▷

Many workers ask the basis of the weighting of the first, second, and third choices. Is one first choice really more important than two, third choices? The answer is that the weighting of scores is purely arbitrary and the scores assigned to the different choices have merely been the ones that the co-researchers with whom we worked have found the most meaningful. You should use the scores which give you the most accurate, useful information. Some research workers have found it makes little difference to score the choices and, therefore, count each choice as one.

While there are many ways of presenting the group's nominations in a picture, the ones illustrated in Figure 4 and Figure 6 are the ones our colleagues have found to be most efficient — shortest time to construct and most information provided. Figure 6 is usually constructed on 8-1/2 x 11 paper which has been divided into four concentric circles. Each circle in the sociogram represents a fourth of the members so that the scores of the members are listed in order and divided into four groups. In our group of 20, five would be in each circle. The members are arranged with the high scorers in the middle, and with as few of the lines showing nominations crossing as is possible.

It may be useful in the sociogram to show specific factors related to member nomination by dividing it into halves or quarters. To highlight male/female factors in choices, the men would be put in one half and the women in the other. In an agency planning committee it might be useful to show the relations of old members and new members as well as male/female. To do this, the sociogram would be divided into quarters as illustrated in Figure 7.

Peer nominations and sociograms can be very exciting to look at and can put social relations into a very alive, action-oriented context. To give them even greater reality and dynamics, photographs of the members are pasted on the sociogram in place of the circles or triangles. In showing a sociogram to members or in

FIGURE 7   *A Sociogram for Old vs. New Members*

Division of a sociogram to show old/new members and male/female relations.

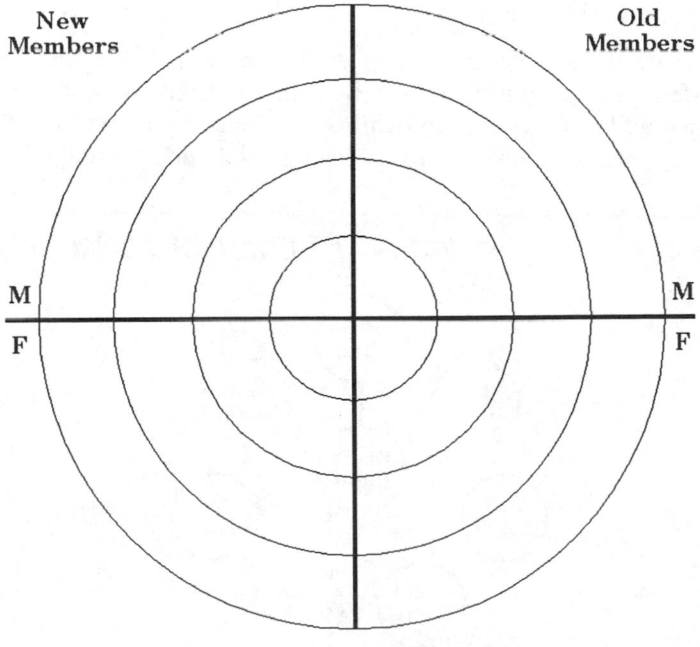

New Members

Old Members

M

F

M

F

using it with other staff, there is a tendency to assess 'nearness to the centre' as the more favoured position and assume they are the more valuable, worthwhile members. This is not meant to be the purpose of a sociogram and, in fact, half in and half out members may provide the linking relationships which hold the group together. There is also a tendency for the creators of the sociogram to become over-enthusiastic about the tool and try to show too much in it. A sociogram that shows three choices for 15 or more people becomes very complicated and turns people off. For this reason we have found a combination of weighted scores and presentation of only first choices, (perhaps two choices in smaller groups), as in Figure 6, to be the most all-around useful presentation.

Presentation of Individual Relationships

Teachers, counsellors, and group workers interested in exploring the unique relationships of individuals will want to look at a separate profile. This could be especially useful with high influence members and problem or deviant members. A separate, individual profile for a high influence member, spotlights the people nominating her who are the members most likely to be influenced by her. And, the nominations of the problem member or deviant member indicate the people who hold some promise of serving as role models or standard setters. A separate chart for Grant Ruple in the Anzacks group looks like the one in Figure 8.

Reciprocal Friendships

The method of establishing acceptance scores for each member was illustrated in Figures 5 and 6, and another score for reciprocal friendships adds additional information. Some members may be well accepted by other members in a group, yet upon analysis of their

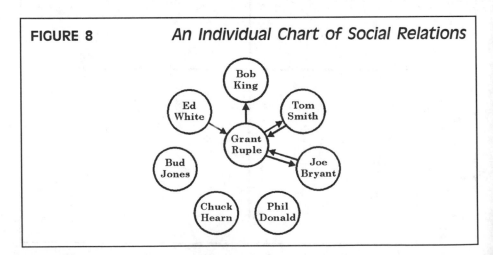

FIGURE 8 *An Individual Chart of Social Relations*

FIGURE 9

Reciprocal Friendship Chart
(in-group choices)

First choice = 5
Second choice = 3
Third choice = 2

Worker: Scudder

Group: Anzacks

Date: May 2nd

Chosen

Last Names	1. Grant Ruple	2. Bob King	3. Tom Smith	4. Joe Bryant	5. Phil Donald	6. Chuck Hearn	7. Bud Jones	8. Ed White
1. Ruple		5	(3)	(2)				
2. King			(3)		(5)			(2)
3. Smith	(5)	(3)					(2)	
4. Bryant	(2)	5						(3)
5. Donald		(5)				(3)	(2)	
6. Hearn					(3)			5
7. Jones			(2)		(3)	5		
8. White	3	(5)		(2)				
Totals	10	23	8	4	11	8	4	10

Chooses

Reciprocal friendships in the Anzacks group.

own choices, it is found that they do not choose the members who have chosen them. A reciprocal friendship is one where each of two members has chosen the other and are identified on the sociogram as a pair. If a person makes three choices, it is possible that all three of those the person chooses may choose him/her in return. If this is the case, there are three reciprocal friendships or a reciprocal friendship score of three. If only two of those the person chose, chose him/her in return, the score would be two, (see Figure 9).

A Group Cohesion Index

One of the best indicators of a group's cohesion is based on the percentage of reciprocal friendships. The formula of group cohesion is the number of mutual friendships divided by the possible number of pairs in the group. Let us take the case of the Anzacks as an example. In looking at Figure 10, we see that there are nine reciprocal friendships in the group. To establish the total number of mutual friendships possible we multiply the maximum number of choices per person — in this case three — by the total number of the group minus one and divide by two.

$$\text{Cohesion} = \frac{\text{Number of mutual friendships}}{\begin{array}{c}\text{Number of possible}\\ \text{mutual friendships}\end{array}} = \frac{9}{3(N-1)/2}$$

$$\text{Cohesion} = \frac{9}{3(8-1)/2} = \frac{9}{3(7)/2} = \frac{9}{21/2} = \frac{9}{10.5} = .857$$

$$\text{Cohesion} = .857$$

The cohesion score of .857 for the Anzacks is very high, as the score would range from zero to one. If this score were expressed in a percentage you might say it was an 86 per cent cohesive group.

An even more meaningful indicator of group cohesion is prepared by allowing members to nominate people who are both inside and outside the group — nominations are not restricted to group members — and then determining the percentage of group members chosen. *Making Workgroups Effective*, described that a group's cohesion was clearly related to the members' attraction to the group. Attraction to a group will be higher where members like and respect the other participants. Thus, if we ask the members of a hockey team to list their ten best friends and eight of Chris' choices are on the team, we would expect her to be more attracted to the team than Dale, who only nominated three other team members. Low attraction scores help to explain absences, lack of enthusiasm for group activities, non-conformity to group standards, and possibly interpersonal difficulties with other members.

A group attraction or cohesion index for the total group can be made by averaging the attraction scores of all the members. Not limiting nominations to group members makes the information more realistic and lifelike. The questions can vary with the type of group.

■ **Social Agency Board**

List the ten people in this city whose opinion it would be most important for you to hear on a social problem concerning local people.

■ **High School Class**

List the five youths that you spend the most time with after school and on weekends.

■ **Any Group**

If we are putting together a steering committee to revitalize our group, (team, department, unit, or whatever), who would be the most important people to have on it? List the names of five you think should be on it.

It has been our experience that such a group attraction index is a very real measure of group cohesion and serves well as a check on cohesion estimated through the group observation procedures described in *How to Observe Your Group*. Our rule of thumb in evaluating group growth is to have three different measures of the group dimension being assessed. In the case of cohesion we have observation and sociometric attraction index as two; the third could be an estimation by the group members themselves. Repeating the same three measures over a period of time would give quite an accurate picture of the group's health related to that dimension.

The Social Relations Scale

Another method of establishing the social acceptance and assessing inclusion of members in a group allows members to rate their liking for every other member of the group. Each member of the group rates the other group members on a five point scale as illustrated in Figure 10. The social relations score of an individual is calculated by counting the number of times others described him/her in the first column, (would like to have him/her as one of my best friends), and multiplying by four, on down to the last column and multiplying by one. This score is then divided by the number of people rating him/her, (total number of the group minus one), with the results ranging from a low of one to a high of five. How well an individual accepts others in the group can be calculated by summing the score of the ratings the person made of other members in the group and dividing by the number of choices made.

The social relations scale has the advantage over a sociometric measure based on three to five choices, in that each member can repeat a feeling about every other member. This may indicate that all members feel very positively about one another, which would not be as clear from a limited choice sociogram. In this way it compares more favourably with an open sociogram, (not restricted to group members). As it is non-threatening and provides well-rounded data, it is our first choice of all the nomination techniques.

The major disadvantage of a social relations index is that it can be less discriminating, (all the members can be lumped in the same box), and the possibility of members being rated as 'not chosen to be in the group' may be more difficult to talk about than simply not being chosen in a forced choice sociogram. The reader may check to see which tells the most about a group by comparing Figure 6 and Figures 10 and 11.

Other Peer Ratings

The term 'member ratings' is used to differentiate ratings based on non-friendship criteria from friendship choices. Research has

FIGURE 10 — Social Relations Check Sheet

Group Ward D Health Care Team   Name Jean Gauthier

Worker Wesley McFee   Date March 6th

Listed below are the other members of the work group. Every one has different ideas about those with whom they work. Check one of the spaces on the right to indicate how you feel about your team's members.

Group Members	Chris Gold	Kim Wlotzka	Cass Adjuti	Lynn Warner	Dale Krikorian	Seto Chan	Kalem Shahed
Very glad to have him/her on the team, and want to work closely with him/her	X	X	X				X
Glad to have him/her on the team, but not as a close associate				X	X	X	
OK to have him/her on the team							
Don't mind having him/her on the team, but don't want much to do with him/her							
I would not choose him/her to be on the team							

Jean rates the other members of the group for the Social Relations Scale.

shown that ratings of group members by other group members are often more accurate in identifying character and leadership qualities than other measures, and they are more practical to carry out. Member ratings, with their high consistency, give a rather true picture of the member being rated. The areas in which people can

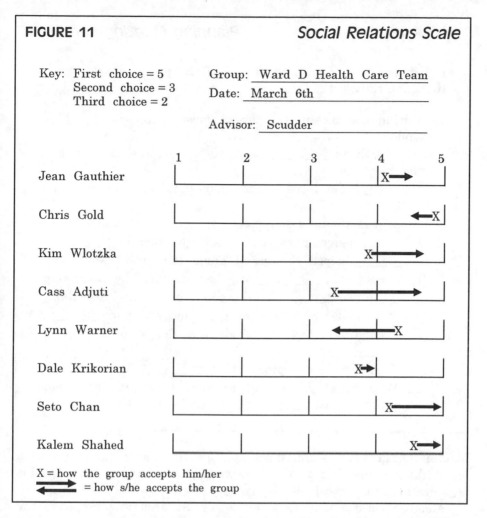

FIGURE 11 *Social Relations Scale*

Key: First choice = 5
      Second choice = 3
      Third choice = 2

Group: Ward D Health Care Team
Date: March 6th

Advisor: Scudder

| | 1 | 2 | 3 | 4 | 5 |
Jean Gauthier
Chris Gold
Kim Wlotzka
Cass Adjuti
Lynn Warner
Dale Krikorian
Seto Chan
Kalem Shahed

X = how the group accepts him/her
= how s/he accepts the group

be rated by others who know them are very broad, but of most interest to human service workers are the areas related to their programs. Thus, ratings usually focus on the personality, perform-ance, skills, and likely behaviour of group members. Or, they ask about changes in behaviour that may be related to participating in the program under study. For example, training programs often ask participants in the program whom they think increased their skills or understanding the most in the program (see Figure 12). Co-workers or people living with the program participants may also be asked to rate them in the relevant areas of performance and skill development. Friends of participants in a training program for disadvantaged youth were asked to assess changes in participants' morale, and parents of youth in a diabetic camp were asked to assess any changes in their child's taking responsibility for the treat-ment of his/her physical condition, such as self-administration of

FIGURE 12   *Planning Meeting Feedback*

Fill in each space with the name of the person in the group that fits the best.

1. During the meeting, I agreed most with what _____ said.
2. Of everybody, _____ seemed to get the most out of the meeting.
3. _____ and I seemed to understand each other pretty well.
4. I felt the group didn't treat _____ very fairly.
5. I couldn't agree much with what was said by _____.
6. _____ helped the group along the most today.
7. It seemed that _____ was not included by the group.
8. _____ and _____ competed most for leadership.
   A. Who is learning the most in this program _____?
   B. Who always has lots of ideas of things to do _____?
   C. Who enjoys the program most _____?
   D. Who would you choose to work with you on a committee of two _____?

insulin. Other peer nominations ask for the names of five people most likely to be able to get a new project off the ground in this organization, (or school, social agency).

Member ratings may focus on a specific area of interest to the group and ask for "the three people most likely to use the learning from this program in their daily life" or "who are the three people in the unit most likely to do agency work on their own time?" Another variation lists a number of things people might do, (volunteer to work on a project, become a big brother or sister, visit a sick member at home, canvass for a concert), and asks members to suggest the names of anybody in the group who would do these things. For children under 12, the list of things people might do can take on a 'guess who' format. "Here is someone who would share candy with another group member — guess who?" The members are then asked to list the names of those in the group, including or excluding themselves, who fit the description.

Another way of handling peer nominations or descriptions is to have all the members rank themselves and all the other members for each item on the list of things people might do (see Figure 13).

FIGURE 13   *Peer Rating/Peer Ranking*

Peer Rating — Health Care Team

Fill in each space with the names of the two people in our Health Care Team that best fits each description.

1. Demonstrates the most patience and understanding with our patients. _____ and _____.
2. Is ready to work extra hard or stay past their shift when things are desperate. _____ and _____.
3. Has a helpful, positive attitude toward their work that inspires others. _____ and _____.
4. Helps other staff out with difficult procedures. _____ and _____.
5. Provides the best all-around care for their patients. _____ and _____.

Peer Ranking — Classroom Assessment

Divide the class into thirds and assign the members to the top, middle, or bottom third of the group on each of the following criteria:

	Top third	Middle third	Lower third
1. Helped us work together as a group.			
2. Contributed most to our assigned work.			
3. Helped to make this experience fun and enjoyable.			
4. Contributed most to my learning something new.			
5. The grade I'd assign based on their performance.			

This approach is most appropriate in a small group, (less than 15), where the member know each other fairly well. In response to a question of 'careful listening' everyone ranks each other and themselves from most to least. This gives a relatively complete and accurate picture of how members see each other. Checking a member's self-ranking against the average of those given by other members shows the accuracy of that person's self-perception. For an

FIGURE 14   *Task Role Summary*

Name: __Bluma Hackett__   ——— Group rating
                                 ▬▬▬ Self rating

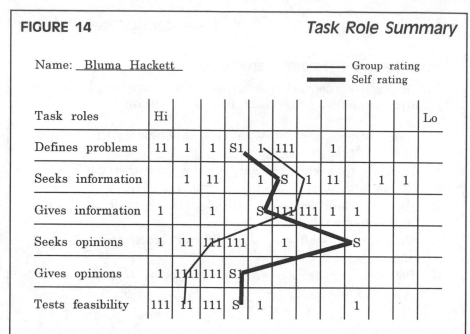

Member rankings of an individual on task roles performed in the group. The solid line shows the average ranking while the thin line is the self-ranking. Each mark 1 represents the ranking by a group member and the S is the self-ranking.

example of this procedure, let's consider its use with the tool **Roles of Group Members**, (*How to Observe Your Group*, pp. 44–45), by a college student executive board. The eleven members of the student board ranked each other on each of the roles described in this tool, from who takes this role most often, to who performs it least often. The results were tabulated by a volunteer following the format of Figure 14 and returned to each member. The results illustrated to the members the roles others saw them performing most and least frequently, compared to the others. And, it showed how accurately they perceived their roles in the group. Figure 14 shows a partial summary, (task roles only), of a member of the executive board. It shows that Bluma has a rather accurate picture of herself as a just above average member in performing task roles, but underestimates her 'opinion seeking' role.

Although the results were returned to the members for their personal use, the group discussed general interpretations. At the next two meetings they practised the roles they wanted to improve and discussed the results at the end of the meeting.

In summary, member ratings give information that is descriptive of an individual and may provide an indication of reputation or social status, competence, and performance level. They do not, compared to sociograms, give much sense of a group's social system or interaction patterns.

Inter-group Sociometric Choices

Often, a group cannot be understood by itself and must be studied in relation to the other groups and people in its environment. The sociometric idea can be easily extended to show the relationship between the two groups, or among several groups. Inter-group sociograms may be constructed along the lines of Figure 7 or some similar method which separates the groups. It can also be useful to extend the sociometric technique and show the relationship and relative status of groups as if they were individuals. Thus, individuals would be asked to nominate other groups or units instead of individuals.

Making Workgroups Effective talked about the value of groups having a well-defined hierarchy where all participants know what is expected of them and what they can expect from each other. Accuracy in perceiving the status and roles of group participants increases the effectiveness of the worker and the members, especially those in key positions. Sociograms clearly showing status hierarchies are constructed from questions such as: 'List in order, the five people in this group to whom you most frequently look to for leadership' or 'Which five members of this group usually determine what is going to happen? — list them in order of influence.'

In summary, it can be said that those people working with groups usually have a pretty good idea from their systematic observations of the interpersonal relationships in their group. Typically, these observation hunches are about 60 per cent accurate with considerable room left for the data provided by a sociogram to improve the accuracy of these observations. When Dimock uses a sociometric measurement, he writes down his predictions of what the results will be, and over the years he has found this to be one of the best professional development experiences to sharpen up his observational skills and check his biases. Sociograms show the important interpersonal dynamics in a group, and when used at two or more points in time, highlight the growth or changes within the group. Above all, sociograms provide the framework for understanding the group behaviour of members that may otherwise seem unexplainable.

Putting Sociometric Data to Work

The information collected through the peer nominations and sociograms usually provides quite a clear picture of where the group stands in handling the inclusion phase of development and indicates the group's status hierarchy, which is so important to a successful resolution of the control stage of development. Informal observations likely provide some hunches of 'who was in' and 'who was out' of the group and the sociogram has made it perfectly clear. Sub-groups and their likely interaction, (bridging member vs. all in group choices), are also clearer. There is also a picture of the membership and acceptance needed to build trust and openness in the group. Future peer ratings and nominations will zero-in on these developmental tasks and focus more on power and influence and goal formation and productivity.

Let's look at a few quick samples of what we might do with the new insights and diagnoses we have derived from these assessments. Detailed descriptions of group analysis and action-planning are found in *Managing Dynamic Groups* and *Intervention and Empowerment: Helping Organizations to Change* — these examples give some closing focus to the sociometric thrust. Attempts to use the new information could start in our usual collaborative style by surfacing the data and turning over the analysis and application of it to the group, (see p. 34, *How to Facilitate the Use of Surveys*). The group or the supervisor/manager could then consider the following:

1. Changing the patterns of groupings or work assignments to increase the participation and interaction of the poorly included members.
2. Increase the visibility and up-front roles of the poorly included by assigning them special tasks.
3. Seek out any special skills or task-related competencies the poorly included may have and try to find an appropriate use for them in the group. Otherwise, arrange external training to upgrade them, (maybe they could become the group's computer consultant or Robert's Rules of Order expert with additional training).
4. Work harder at increasing the range of individual differences the group will accept.
5. Use the high status/high acceptance people as team leaders for group projects.
6. Pair them, (as peer helpers or coaches), with low status members, where appropriate.
7. Have potentially isolated sub-groups collaborate on a project, the success of which requires their full cooperation.
8. Consider using the supervisor or external resources for individual counselling and coaching with isolated or rejected members.

As the developmental tasks of inclusion and acceptance are accomplished, not only will the group's performance quickly improve, but it will have the solid base needed to become a fully functioning group. Otherwise, a group with unresolved inclusion will always be in trouble.

Other Data Collection Methods

Needs Assessments and Interest Surveys

One of the most frequently used tools to gather information about a group is an interest survey, (see Figure 15). It may be called a needs analysis, an interest census, (Figure 16), or a program locator, as it identifies programs, activities, or work procedures that are desired by the members. The survey may take the form of a check-off sheet with a list of interests or activities and participants are asked to check those that are of interest and double check the most important items. Members may also be asked to list or

---

FIGURE 15　　　*Interest Survey (Teen Group, abridged)*

Read each activity and put a check mark (✓) beside those you have participated in sometime in the past year. Underline those activities you'd like to do.

- [ ] helping the troop produce a play.
- [ ] making a sculpture with wood or clay.
- [ ] setting up a weather station at a campout.
- [ ] making a model of the solar system.
- [ ] helping to plan activities for the troop.

- [ ] organizing a patrol as a patrol leader.
- [ ] learning about physical fitness.
- [ ] organizing a bicycle safety course.
- [ ] learning about black music.
- [ ] learning how to patent an invention.

FIGURE 16　　　*Needs and Interest Census*
— Board of Education

1. What do you think are the most important needs of the board at this time to help it function more effectively?
2. What would help you do your job as a trustee more successfully?
3. What would you like to work on, as a special interest, in the next three months?
4. What do you think would help us work together more effectively as a board?
5. What kind of training would interest you personally?

---

to check the expectations they have for the group. Such a list might include:

- make new friends.
- improve physical fitness.
- feel better about myself.
- work on a service project.
- learn new skills.
- travel to different places.

Such surveys provide a clear picture of what a group wants to do together and general expectations for its membership. This information is valuable in understanding why members are in the group, what is motivating them, and what will help them become more involved. Re-doing a needs analysis at a second point in time provides valuable data to estimate group growth through comparisons.

Interest groups are also a rich source of data about the individuals who compose a group. They can be used to tell if people have:

1. interests more or less mature compared to their age group; or typical interests considering sex, geographical location, education, and ethnic and religious affiliation.
2. preferences for a kind of activity such as hard/soft, spectator/active, structured/creative, self-directed/leader led, individual/group, or competitive/cooperative.
3. interests congruent to those of the program or values similar to those of the agency. And, the extent to which interests and values become more congruent measures the impact of program participation.

The most useful interest surveys are 'home grown' to fit a specific group and situation and the above examples should help you to make up your own. Charting the changing interests of individuals, groups, and staff teams is a powerful method of assessing the effectiveness of human service programs.

Attitude and Personality Surveys

There are hundreds of attitude and personality surveys available for a variety of purposes.[1] They represent a broad range of areas

---

1   John Robinson, Paul Shaver, and Lawrence Wrightsman (eds.). *Measures of Personality and Social Psychological Attitudes.* New York: Academic Press, 1990. J.W. Pfeiffer (ed.) *Theories and Models in Applied Behavioural Science* (4 vols.), San Diego: Peiffer & Co., 1991. *Instrumentation Kit* (3 Vols.). San Diego: Peiffer & Co., 1988.

and it is usually easier to use one that has been carefully prepared and its usefulness established than to make up one of your own.

Typical areas of focus of the available inventories and surveys include:

- moral judgement and values.
- locus of control.
- personal rigidity.
- trust and acceptance of others.
- socio-political attitudes.
- various personality traits.
- social issues and problems.
- use of coping behaviours.
- sexual orientation and behaviour.
- attitudes toward working in a group.
- self-esteem.
- alienation.
- attitudes towards authority.
- social sensitivity.
- religious attitudes.
- family relations.
- ethnic and religious groups.
- styles of leadership.
- interest inventories.
- perception of our roles in a group.

Personal Data from Members

Many organizations routinely collect basic personal information when starting work with a new program participant, volunteer, or worker. This 'face sheet' type information usually includes name, age, sex, address and telephone number, marital status, education, place of employment, and so on. While some of these personal areas have recently been excluded through humans rights legislation, many organizations continue to record extensive information about their clients. In some organizations, (health units, colleges, social services, and special needs programs), this information is supplemented with either a selection intake interview or an extensive written questionnaire. It may also include a needs assessment, (what are the present problems that need help?), or in the case of a college, volunteer job, or recreation department, an interest survey asking how the participant wants to use the resources available. These records are often overlooked as a very rich source of information that can assist in understanding participants and planning for the full utilization of their skills and resources. They also form a baseline profile which is useful in evaluating individual and group growth.

Autobiographics and diaries are also a useful and sometimes readily available source of information for understanding individual members and analyzing groups. Many educational and training programs require an autobiography for admission. In some of the group research we have designed, we have asked participants about themselves, their families, friends, and interests. We were overwhelmed with the quality and depth of information presented. In human services we don't want to spend our time collecting tons of data we won't use, hence, our rule of thumb is to keep the statement very short, and increase its relevance by asking a few leading questions, such as the ones above.

A more easily used form is an autobiographical episode report form such as, 'what is the most important part of your life right now', 'talk a bit about the most important experience in your life', or 'describe the people in your life whom you have admired the most'.

During their teens, boys and especially girls keep diaries of their activities, thoughts, and personal reactions to people and situations. College and university students may keep learning logs. Adults keep appointment calendars. Program participants may share the records they have or start keeping specific information, if they are sure the information will be useful to their group or future programs.

Other self-reports take the form of asking members to describe 'their three wishes' or 'what you would like to be doing three years from now'. Youth may be asked to describe 'what I did last summer' or 'the person in my life I admire the most'. There are also a number of commercial self-report inventories on the market that collect much of the same data but in a more systematic way and generally with some kind of scoreable, comparable outcomes.

Member Reports on Programs

Member reactions to group situations and activities are just as accurate and useful a source of information as the member reactions and ratings of each other described in the earlier part of this section. This useful source of data is often overlooked in the belief that the members don't know very much about what is really going on in the group. However, member reactions usually give a more reliable and often a truer picture of the group's situation than does an evaluation by the supervisor. Probably the most natural way for members to supply information on their reactions to the group is through a descriptive, narrative writing, diary, or focused vignette. Very often a group has a recorder whose job it is to write up a record of the meeting. This may supply some information but it is usually not personal enough — doesn't tell how the writer felt or how the others seemed to feel — to give a comprehensive picture. In order to provide more than a factual account of a meeting or group activity, a group can use two people to prepare records. One tells what happened, what decisions or plans were made, and is a **content** record, (perhaps kept by the group recorder). The other is a **process** report and tells how things happened, giving hunches about how members felt in connection with observations of their

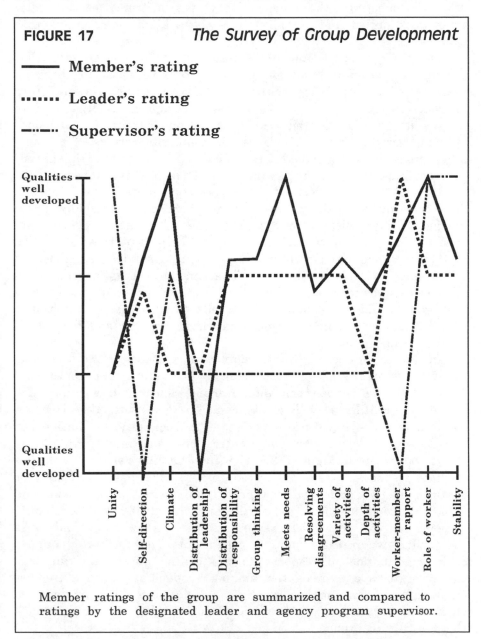

FIGURE 17   *The Survey of Group Development*

——— Member's rating

······· Leader's rating

—··—·· Supervisor's rating

Member ratings of the group are summarized and compared to ratings by the designated leader and agency program supervisor.

individual behaviour. This is a personal report, more in the stance of a group observer.

Focused anecdotes or vignettes are rich and exciting sources of group information and a well-established method of program evaluation, (Patton, 1980). Members are asked to record a short vignette describing what was most interesting, surprising, or important to them in the group that day. Or, in what we call the 'meeting after the meeting', the members have an informed session after their work period and verbally share these kinds of reactions with each other.

Many of the observation tools described in *How to Observe Your Group*, can be used by group members to give focus to their assessment of the group. The **Survey of Group Development**, (*How to Observe Your Group*, p. 41–43), was designed for this kind of use as it gives an overview of a group on the major dimensions of group growth. Figure 17 shows the composite ratings of a young adult group by its members, its designated leader, and the agency program supervisor on the **Survey of Group Development**.

It is particularly worthwhile to take some time toward the end of a meeting or activity and ask members either verbally or in writing to give their reactions. The 'end of meeting reports' and 'post meeting reaction forms', (PMR's), can help focus these reactions, and by comparing the results from session to session, progress can be assessed. Members can also be asked to discuss or report on such basic questions as: problems we had in our group today; how the group could have improved its effectiveness; important things that happened that not everyone may have noticed; and how I felt in the group today.

In our experience, leaders report a very strong commitment to conducting some kind of post meeting evaluation, but continually report that the session ran into overtime and there was no time to do the P.M.R. they had planned. To deal with this common concern, (and we have also experienced it frequently), a contingency P.M.R. was developed by our Centre. The one minute P.M.R. is shown below, (see Figure 18). The five minute version, with immediate feedback to any size group up to 100, has the facilitator putting the two scales on newsprint, chalkboard, or overhead, and explaining their meaning. All participants are then asked to identify a point on the scale that represents their assessment and raise their hand when that point is called out. The facilitator quickly counts the hands in response to the calling out of the numbers from one to five, records the number responding to each number on the chart, and makes a quick calculation of the average on each scale to sum up the meeting. This is a big winner for which there is always time.

FIGURE 18   *Post Meeting Reaction*

One-minute Post Meeting Reaction

1. How well did we do today in accomplishing our task? (circle the point on the scale that most nearly represents your opinion).

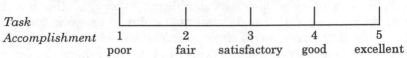

Task Accomplishment

| 1 | 2 | 3 | 4 | 5 |
| poor | fair | satisfactory | good | excellent |

2. How well did we do today in working as a group and building our relationships?

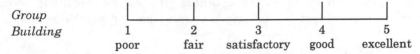

Group Building

| 1 | 2 | 3 | 4 | 5 |
| poor | fair | satisfactory | good | excellent |

Post Meeting Reaction (five-minute)

1. How helpful did you find this meeting? (circle one)

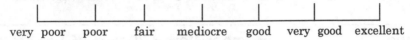

| very poor | poor | fair | mediocre | good | very good | excellent |

2. What were the major strengths of the meeting?
3. What were the major weaknesses?
4. What do you think should be done next?

P.M.R. (training and counselling sessions)

1. To what extent did this session deal with your real concerns?

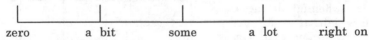

| zero | a bit | some | a lot | right on |

2. What things did you not say that you might have?
3. What do you see yourself doing differently after this session?
4. What issue or topic do you want to work on next?

Evaluation Form (steering committee)

1. How clear did you feel we were about our goals? (circle one)

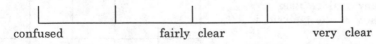

| confused | fairly clear | very clear |

2. How cooperatively did we work?

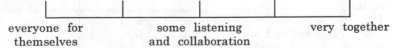

| everyone for themselves | some listening and collaboration | very together |

3. What do you suggest to improve the productivity of the group?

Reports from Others

Useful information about a group or about its members can be collected from people close to the group or its members. They may be participants in other programs in the agency with whom this group interacts or they may be 'significant others' of the members such as spouses, special friends, parents, siblings, or work colleagues. Students usually have very clear pictures of what they think of the other classes they are not taking and those 'others' living with a program member are astute observers of changes in behaviour, attitudes, or skills of that member as they surface in the daily living setting. To be sure, these others provide an excellent second opinion about any group analysis the group or its worker is making.

Peer Group Norms

Peer groups quickly establish norms or usual ways of doing things in a group. These norms are built on the values members bring to the group and establish as a group. It is the culture of

---

FIGURE 19   *Member Norms (Board of Directors)*

check one box for each statement

How many feel this way?

	all	most	half	some	a few
1. It is good to take part as much as possible in our board meetings.					
2. It is helpful to suggest new initiatives for the board rather than just react to the set agenda.					
3. Extra long meetings help us feel we have really done our job and have contributed to this organization.					
4. It is generally inappropriate to express any real emotion or say how we feel about a topic.					
5. It's ok to be absent one in every four meetings.					
6. Our role is to make policy decisions and we shouldn't get involved in or discuss staff relations problems.					

How many people in this ☐ group ☐ organization would do the following? Check one box for each item.

	most	some	a few	no one
1. Suggest a new idea or approach for doing things.				
2. Go out of his/her way to help another member.				
3. Listen to others and try to get their opinions.				
4. Do the least amount of work to get by.				
5. Ask the supervisor for special help on a problem.				
6. Try to get ahead by putting other members down.				
7. Work harder than necessary just to do a good job.				
8. Try to get people to work together for the common good.				
9. Talk openly about problems.				
10. Try to reduce costs when 'freebies' are available.				

the group and is a composite of the perceptions members have about what is appropriate to do in the group. What the members think the norms are, is what influences their behaviour and these become the group standards. It is helpful to document these group standards or usual ways of doing things and descriptions by the members provide the most reliable information.

In *How to Observe Your Group*, (Figure 9, p. 28), a **Culture Analysis Observation Guide** was presented and it can be used just as well as a member report form. A number of other observation suggestions were made on the following two pages to learn more about a group's culture.[2] Figure 19 shows a sample of another approach to assessing the perceptions of members about the norms and values in the group. It is a survey that is especially useful to collate, and board or distribute the total group's resources as the focus of a discussion. Two outcomes of such a group discussion are likely: members find out there is no agreement about what the standards are, and, the group may choose to modify or change some of the norms. Figure 20 depicts another sample of a survey used to assess norms.

---

2   A further discussion of group culture analysis is found in Dimock, *Intervention and Empowerment: Helping Organizations to Change*, 1993 p. 34–38. It includes an observation guide and a member questionnaire.

How to Facilitate the Use of Surveys

Using surveys with a group involves seven steps:

1. Introduction and climate setting.
2. Rationale for the survey's use.
3. Completing the survey and creating group results.
4. Sharing (displaying) group results.
5. Analysis of results by the group.
6. Implications and theory building.
7. Integration — individual and group.

Our approach to the use of surveys, (nominations, self descriptions, peer assessments, group ratings), is that they are tools to help group members understand themselves, their role in the group, and the overall dynamics of the group in order to enhance their personal growth and the group's development and success. This means that the surveys or instruments have to be owned and operated by the group — not someone doing something to or for the group. An accepting, non-evaluative climate needs to be established. Support between and among members can be built in by having members pair up or form triads for the activity. The overall schedule for these activities, perhaps with some time lines, should also be presented in the introduction so that members know where they are going and what is expected of them.

Secondly, the rationale for the use of this particular survey should be presented to the group; why it was chosen and where it came from. Our preference is to have a small task group either prepare a 'home grown' survey or select an existing survey and modify it for the group's use. See Figure 21 for a sample 'home grown' survey used in an educational setting. They then present the survey, describe where it came from, and explain the rationale for its use. This may include a bit of theoretical background, (the role of inclusion in group development), and a prediction of how the survey may help the group. Questions and reactions may surface at this time as the group takes more ownership over the activity. The group then decides to go ahead with the activity — buy in — or sends it back for more task group work.

In the third phase of the activity, the group completes the survey and makes arrangements for collating data and creating the desired group results. This would likely be done by the task group if it is in place. Or, it may be practical for the group to board or tabulate the information as a total group.

Once the data is boarded, or all the members have copies of the results, the group moves into a discussion led by the facilitator

FIGURE 21

Assessment of Power and Influence in the System (college or university)

How much power and influence do you think the following groups have in determining the operation of this college/university? (admission, staffing, curriculum, academic standards, student activities, etc.) Check one box for each group.

	a great deal	a lot	some	little or none
1. Board of Governors.				
2. Chancellor.				
3. Principal/President.				
4. Deans.				
5. Department Chairs/ Academic Directors.				
6. Student Council.				
7. Faculty Council or Senate.				
8. Alumni.				
9. Faculty.				
10. Students.				
11. Association of Colleges/Universities.				
12. Provincial Government.				
13. Federal Government.				
14. Student Services (guidance, student life, and athletics).				
15. Faculty/Staff Union.				
16. Student Lobby Groups.				
17. Media (McLean's Ratings etc.).				
18. Community Groups, Schools and Organizations.				

or designated leader. This analysis and interpretation of the survey data may be fairly structured, using the theoretical framework supporting the survey or a spontaneous 'eyeballing'. The important function of the facilitator at this stage is to surface all the likely interpretations and legitimize them, (there are no 'right' answers and there are many possible interpretations of the data). This phase may also be enhanced by using the pairs or triads to work up their analysis and then report back to the total group.

Following the analysis and interpreting phase, the facilitator leads the group into an exploration of the possible implications of the analysis for the group. "So what does all this mean for our group?" This may include a review of the theoretical framework for the survey and modifying it or building on it using the results and interpretations from the group.

Integration of the activity includes helping individuals clarify their learnings from the activity and checking what, if anything, they think they should do about it. The group should also review the possible implications for the group and decide what, if anything, they choose to do about it. Closure is established with a general debriefing and evaluation of the experience.

PART TWO

Assessing Individual and Group Development

Thorndike once said that anything that exists, exists in some amount, and that amount can be measured. Human behaviour has been very difficult to measure, yet in recent years the behavioural sciences have made great advances in assessing both individual and group growth.

Many group programs are like a merry-go-round. There is action, excitement, and fun, but the participants get off right where they got on. There has been a lot of activity but everyone ends up just where they started. To prevent programs from becoming merry-go-rounds, there need to be clearly stated, measurable goals, and regular assessment of movement toward these goals. It is this process that separates educational and recreational programs from those that are just occupying peoples' time.

The rapidly increasing percentage of all money that is spent on human service programs — education, social welfare, recreation, and health services — has accelerated the expectation that these programs would provide some objective evidence of the usefulness of their work. Usually, there is a direct relationship between the quality of a human service program and its efforts to systematically assess the impact of its work in relation to its stated goals.

The most important function of group appraisals is to help the group and the designated leader understand the factors affecting their efforts to improve the group's operation. Many of the observation guides, sociometric devices, and rating scales described here and in *How to Observe Your Group*, can be used with little additional effort to measure group growth. A measurement design may do nothing more than plan to use the information collected from the regular use of these tools in a comparative way to show changes within the group. The methods and procedures described here to measure individual and group growth can be used by staff who have not had research and statistical training. More advanced methods of program evaluation involving statistical and qualitative analysis of more carefully collected group data can be found in the *Simplified Guide to Program Evaluation* title in this series.

Reliability, Validity, and Statistical Significance

These terms, frequently used in measurement, are useful ones for the designated leader to understand. The term **reliability** refers to the degree that a repeated measure by the same procedure gives similar results. For example, a twelve inch ruler is usually very reliable as a tool to measure the width of a desk. A piece of string would be a much less reliable measuring tool for the same purpose as it is subject to stretching. A reliable measuring tool should also be accurate and precise. Suppose you wanted to find the length of time it takes sound to travel one mile. If you made several tests and timed each one with a stopwatch, calibrated in fractions of seconds, you would be much more likely to get the same answer than if you used a wristwatch. Both watches are reliable but the stopwatch is more precise and can be read more accurately. Before we can measure anything we must have reasonably reliable measurement tools.

The term **validity** refers to the extent a measurement produces relevant information about the subject being measured. Does the test or tool measure what we want it to measure? This is the question raised in seeking validity. The more valid an instrument is, the more it is able to predict what it is we want to know. A ruler is considered to be a very valid tool for linear measurement as it will predict whether our desk will fit through a given doorway.

Statistical significance tells the likelihood of there being a real, non-chance change between two measurements. Change within a group over a period of time may be due to chance changes or normal fluctuations within the group. A test of statistical significance is needed to determine the likelihood that the change is not due to these factors. A study of the weight of ten people may show an average gain of half a pound in two weeks. A test of significance gives the worker an indication of whether this was due to chance changes and inaccuracies in measurement or, whether it indicated an actual weight gain on the part of the people.

While the terms reliability, validity, and statistical significance are in constant use in almost all of the program evaluation reports, they do not meet our needs. We are interested in improving the programs we lead and in helping our organization establish priorities among its various programs in relation to the achievement of organization goals. First and foremost, we want assessment information that we and our groups can use to increase our effectiveness. Hopefully it will also help our organizations determine our contribution to what they are trying to do. Hence, our first criterion is **utilization**. Secondly, we want information about group growth that is **credible**, that people can believe is a true representation of the group. Group assessments are likely to be more accurate if they are **confirmable** and our rule of thumb is to try to triangulate important aspects of our measurements by looking at the same aspect from three different viewpoints. For example, indicators of a group's cohesion could come from observations, sociograms, and group records. Or, if the most practical source of the data is from observations, then they should come from another agency staff member or a visitor. These three criteria fit together and build on each other, for the more confirmable the measurements are, the more likely they will be seen as credible and trustworthy, and the more trust and confidence people have in the data, the more likely they are to use it in group planning.

What Can be Evaluated

In general, there are three different kinds of things that can be measured in a program to analyze and evaluate individual and group growth.

1. Changes in behaviour, lifestyle, or well-being of individual members in their daily lives.
2. Changes in knowledge, sensitivity, attitudes, self-understanding, and skills of members as they relate to program goals.
3. Changes in the group dimensions related to growth such as climate, involvement, interaction, cohesion, and productivity. The developmental level or stage of group growth can also be assessed. This could be extended to include evaluations of group composition, content, leadership, and activities in relation to the stated goals and objectives for the group.

Agency goals often expect their programs will change the behaviour of participants in their daily lives, yet in practice, staff rarely evaluate it. Participants report in some kind of program follow-up what they think they are doing differently. Or, their co-workers, family, and friends may be asked to describe the changes they have noted which may be related to participating in the agency's program. This area is usually given to outside researchers/evaluators if it is studied, and has little to do with day-to-day program planning.

Most human service evaluation looks at changes in participant's knowledge, attitudes, and skills, or at changes in group dimensions and related program information. Technical skills such as physical strength and endurance, or artistic, musical, or mechanical skills are a focus of evaluation activities. This is the usual approach to school subjects. Our culture shows a keen interest in what people know and what they can do.

Other Measures of Group and Agency Goals

Membership figures and other indirect appraisals are frequently used to evaluate group programs. Some indirect measures are fairly useful while others are quite doubtful. Figures of the gross number of people served or yearly attendance records tell very little. They may show an increase from one year to the next and this suggests

39

that the agency is popular. Any large movie theatre could probably report larger attendance and by the same token should be considered more popular. If the attendance figures are used to imply effectiveness in servicing the community, the theatre would have to be given credit for doing a 'better job'. Attendance figures that are broken down to indicate the number of hours a month members spent in agency programs and the turnover of members have more meaning. A further breakdown into age groups shows if the agency is working with the groups to achieve its goals and policies.

Membership statistics, attendance in different programs, and program content give information about agency organization, but tell nothing about the achievement of specific goals. The number of members in large and small groups, with a ratio of staff or advisors to these groups, is more important for there is evidence to show that personal growth and specific skills, such as swimming, are best achieved in small groups. Small groups or classes, with appropriate leadership are important, but this in itself does not mean that members are growing and developing, only that there is a greater probability of them doing so.

An analysis of program content indicates that there is a logical connection between the program and the agency goals. An agency with physical education goals builds its program around the learning and practice of a variety of physical skills and the practice of good health habits. An informal education agency builds its program around group experiences where new behaviour and values can be learned, discussed, and practised in the program. A review of program content and the percentage of members participating in different activities helps an agency check the degree to which its program is planned with agency objectives in mind.

Making Workgroups Effective, described research studies which showed a relationship between the leader's personality and style of leadership, and the behaviour and growth of members in their group. The research suggested that participative, group-centred leaders were more likely than dominating, directive leaders, to have healthy groups and positive member growth. The study of these aspects of leadership has been a popular indirect measure of goal achievement potential in different situations.

Utilization Focused Assessments

The assessments made of individual and group growth have, as their purpose, the improvement of the effectiveness of the group. Thus, a useful appraisal clarifies areas where improvements can be made. Occasionally, an evaluation of two or more programs will help a worker or an agency establish where time and money are best spent, but most of the time the focus is on improving the program. Especially important in these attempts to analyze and evaluate group growth are tentative answers to the questions that will guide the worker's intervention and organization planning (size of group, length and frequency of meetings, program focus, communication with other groups, productivity level, etc.).

From our many years of experience in helping hundreds of human service organizations, a few principles have emerged for increasing the likelihood that appraisal activities will help the group become more effective.

1. Whatever is done should be done on a regular on-going basis.
2. Everyone should know what is going to happen and, if appropriate, be involved in the assessment activity (observing, doing peer nominations, keeping records, collating and analyzing data, or wherever they can help). The greater the group's involvement, the greater the probability of the assessment leading to action planning and implementation.
3. Keep the assessment simple and easy to manage.
4. Quality not quantity is the goal. Piaget, the world famous French psychologist, rarely studied more than ten children in any project.
5. Select critical incidents, seminal events, special situations, or individuals for more in-depth study.
6. Try to have multiple perspectives, (triangulation), for all important areas.

Time and again, in our evaluation activities we have found that if people are presented with very credible data by a group worker, (and especially an outsider), they were not likely to make use of it even if the implications were clear and related to the group's concerns. But, if the same information was collected by group members the data was more likely to be discussed and used for future activities. Out of these experiences came our new approach to increasing the effectiveness of groups and organizations called Systems Improvement Research,[3] grounded on the principle of member collaboration in the assessment and improvement of activities.

Assessment Designs

To appraise the results of a program there needs to be a design or plan to collect relevant information, a selection of the methods and tools to collect the information, and some method of analyzing

---

3   H. Dimock, *Intervention and Empowerment: Helping Organizations to Change*. North York, ON: Captus Press, 1993. For U.S. Edition, see H. Dimock, *Intervention and Collaboration: Helping Organizations to Change*. San Diego, CA: Pfeiffer & Co., 1993.

and interpreting the information. Let's turn to the first of these considerations.

The purpose of the assessments described here is to improve the effectiveness of the group. To do this, the group, and more especially, the staff worker or designated leader needs to understand what is happening in the group and why. There is a need to know the basis of program successes and how they can be built on and made even more successful. Program criteria are always in terms of strengths and weaknesses and not judgments such as fair, good, or excellent.

The Preferred Design

The single best design for collecting this relevant information is on an on-going, regular basis rather than before and after. Collecting and perhaps analyzing the data are part of the regular activities of the group. This design is called a 'time lapse design' which means that the data collection takes place at regular time intervals. This is the normal practice in many groups where attendance is taken at each session and there is some record or 'minutes' of the meeting. The recruitment of new members takes place at regular times and is followed with orientation and indoctrination activities. The one addition that would be new for many groups in using a time lapse design is including a follow-up measurement or questionnaire after a member has departed or the group has terminated. The addition of a follow-up measurement shortly after the program has concluded or several members have left, identifies the permanency of any change resulting from the program.

The 'after only' design is very familiar to us as most of our educational experiences included a final exam in school and a program evaluation in informal educational programs. While these end of program evaluations are quite easy to perform, they don't provide a lot of information about the program. As they aren't done until the end of the program, they can't be used to improve that program.

Before and After Designs

The most useful designs for program evaluation are extensions of good program planning procedures. Most community recreation programs are built around the assessed needs and interests of community participants, and a practical evaluation design would see repeating the assessment at a later point in time and checking on how well the needs were being met. The beginning of a school year often includes establishing the reading and math level of the students to assist the educator in planning appropriate level work. These tests can be repeated half way through the year to determine what progress has been made. Most counselling programs commence with the taking of a case history which lists the client's symptoms, problems, and major worries. Repeating the case history by way of updating any changes at a later point in time can highlight progress by comparing the symptoms, problems, and worries. The place to start your planning is with what you are presently doing with your programs, and consider doing some of your data collection twice. This will give you material that you can compare to assess the impact of the program.

Control Group Designs

Everyone who watches television may recall the Crest toothpaste ads of the 1970's describing the differences in tooth decay between the experimental group, (Crest), and the control group, (Brand X), and you may be wondering why this design hasn't been mentioned. Well, it's still the ideal design but a lot has happened since then. First, everyone knows about Brand X and doesn't want to have anything to do with it. And, most workers in the human service area are increasingly concerned about human rights and feel it's unethical or inappropriate to leave people out of a service they want or need — and especially to pretend that they are getting it. Second, it isn't necessary to have a control group that receives 'no treatment' to accurately evaluate a program. Third, a lot of progress has been made during these years in refining evaluation tools and methods and in understanding what really helps to improve programs — this has made control groups both less popular and less necessary for program development.

To the extent that it is necessary to have a very rigorously controlled evaluation, a control group may still be used, but an equally useful design without the drawbacks mentioned above goes as follows. The program or group to be studied is identified ahead of time and the participants are measured *before* they enter the program. As they enter the program, they repeat the measurements and are measured a third time at the end of the program. The difference between the first and second measurements serves as the 'control group', for they did not participate in the program under study during that time. The difference between the second and third measurements established what impact, if any, the program under study had on them. If this difference is greater than what took place between the first and second control measurements, then it can be assumed that the difference is likely related to participating in the program.

A while back, our Centre was consulting with two high schools as they introduced leadership training and human relations courses for their students, one for credit and one non-credit. Both school boards wanted some pretty hard data about the effectiveness of these programs and we used the design of measuring the students likely to participate the same amount of time before the program started as they were in the program. The students who took the course for five months were measured five months before the course started, the first day of the course and during the next to last week of the course, (so the results could be reported to them in the last week). This gave us comparable data on the amount of growth taking place through regular school activities and that occurring during the period students were taking the new course. In both schools, students continued to grow and develop, but in one school the change was similar to what had taken place in the previous length of time. An extra attraction of this design was that all the students were very interested in getting individual reports on their progress and this helped them to assess their own learning in comparison with other students.

Methods of Collecting Information

There are five ways of collecting data that can be used to evaluate the program. The selection of the most appropriate method depends on the importance of the assessment, (time and energy people are prepared to put into it), and on what fits into usual program activities. Those who are doing the program appraisal should also select an approach that is comfortable for them and one that interests them.

1. **Self reports** — you can ask the people, (participants and workers), about themselves, their experiences, and about each other.
2. **Reports from others** — you can ask others who know the participants or the group about them and their experiences.
3. **Direct observations** — you can observe the participants, the group at work, and its interaction with other groups.
4. **Performance outcomes** — you can test the participants and workers; do clinical exams; collect physical, financial, employment data, or monitor measurable performance of the group.
5. **Review program and operation records** — you can check budget allocations, program schedules, job assignments, policy making records, and general unit and community records.

- **Written Information Tests**

Tests of knowledge and understanding are used to ascertain how much of the program information members have picked up and assimilated. These tests are common in many educational programs. Similar tests may be handled verbally rather than in writing.

- **Written Questionnaires or Surveys**

Measures of attitudes, beliefs, personal orientation or interests. The **Dimock Leadership Inventory** is typical of these

44

tools, as are the numerous surveys of values, temperament, and personality.[4]

Post meeting reactions. Figure 18 (page 31) shows typical samples of these. The forms ask participants to give reactions to a specific meeting or program session. While it is usually conducted as a written questionnaire, it can also be done verbally. In a large group, two or three rating scales may be noted on a chalkboard and participants asked to raise their hands on the point on the scale they choose when it is called out. Or, if there is coffee after the program, three or four interviewers can move about asking the post-meeting questions and gain a pretty good sampling of responses.

Needs assessments and interest finders. These surveys have been described and ask members to list their interests or concerns in various areas related to the program. Alternatively, a comprehensive list of interests or concerns may be provided and members are asked to check off the ones that apply.

Inter-group, organizational, or environmental scans or surveys. These will be discussed in the next section of the book.

- ■ **Self Reports**
- • **Personal information sheet.**
- • **Autobiographical sketches.**
- • **Diaries, learning logs,** or **critical incident reports.**

■ **Descriptions and Ratings of Members**

These may be self-ratings or descriptions, or they may be completed by other members or staff. They may be extended to include friends, family, or coworkers. Rating scales, standardized case studies for comparative purposes, anecdotal records or behaviour descriptions, and critical incidents may be used to give greater meaning to these descriptions.

■ **Peer Nominations and Sociograms**

Participants can be asked to nominate members to fill various categories such as team leader, social convenor, or 'someone who gets things done'. The use of sociometric choices and the social relations index which have been extensively described are popular choices in this category. They can be used to analyze the social structure of the group and establish levels of group cohesion and attraction to the group, which can then be used as indicators of group growth.

---

4   John Robinson, Paul Shaver, and Lawrence Wrightsman (eds.). *Measures of Personality and Social Psychological Attitudes.* New York: Academic Press, 1990. J.W. Pfeiffer (ed.) *Theories and Models in Applied Behavioural Science* (4 vols.), San Diego: Peiffer & Co., 1991. *Instrumentation Kit* (3 Vols.). San Diego: Peiffer & Co., 1988.

■ Group Records

Records kept by the group recorder, minutes kept by a secretary, and the worker's records provide considerable information about attendance, how the group spent its time and plans for the future. They may also highlight what was accomplished and levels of members' participation. The attendance record shows the stability of the group and notes who is absent with what frequency, as well as the rate of turnover in the group.

■ Descriptions or Ratings of Group Operation

These descriptions can be made by the members or staff, or perhaps by visitors or independent observers. The **Survey of Group Development** and other rating forms have been shown as illustrations in *How to Observe Your Group.* Another example of use of the **Survey of Group Development** is included at the end of the previous section.

■ Projective Descriptions of the Group

Information is collected from these techniques by exposing the members to a general stimulus to which they may respond in different ways. Members may be asked, for example, to draw a picture of the group. People in residential programs can be asked to draw a picture of the organization, (camp, residence, or institution). Old magazines can be given to members who are asked to make a collage of cut out pictures representing the group or perhaps their role in the group. Members can also be asked to put on a skit depicting the group or role play recent critical situations. Creating songs, poems, or fables about the group are productive projective methods.

■ Systematic Observations

This is the most frequently used method of group appraisal, as everyone is always observing what is going on. The only problem is to make the observation systematic and confirmable. *How to Observe Your Group* describes the procedures and observation guides to upgrade the quality of observations. Several years of perfecting group observations in the Systems Improvement Research project found that the use of two observers — one of whom was a member of the group and the other an outside independent observer — was the most favourable approach, (the best data for the least amount of time).

■ Video Recordings

With the common ownership of camcorders, most groups have access to equipment to video record their group sessions. Groups are often excited about this extension of the observation method as members may not have seen themselves in 'the movies' before. While the novelty quickly wears off, the enthusiasm to watch and discuss a session is a powerful stimulant for an analysis and appraisal of a group's operation. The advantage of a video recording is the opportunity it provides members to observe themselves interacting within the group. The feedback received from this kind of self-analysis may be more useable and have more impact than feedback received from others. Video recordings are also particularly useful in documenting the life of a group over a period of time so that the group can review its progress by comparing the visual records.

■ **Interviews**

Individual and group interviews are another way of collecting the information described under: written questionnaires or surveys; self-reports; descriptions, nominations, and sociometric choices; and descriptions or ratings of group operation. It has been our experience that interviewing is worth the additional time in situations where the interviewer wants to build a relationship with the respondent, such as a group leader or board chairperson interviewing a new group member. Or where part of, or a whole group, can be interviewed and the participants will learn as much useful information from each other as will the interviewer. The other situation where interviews have been found to be appropriate is in program follow-ups where not all respondents will take the time to complete a written questionnaire. Here, an interview, especially a telephone interview, makes it possible and cost-effective to hear from all the participants.

■ **Simulations, Role Playing and Virtual Experience**

Case problems have been used to some extent, where group members are given some information about a situation and asked how they would handle it. These cases may be presented in written form, in film or video, through a role play or demonstration, or by having the person involved in the situation come and verbally present it to the group. In our leadership training programs we use written case studies: videos such as, *Twelve Angry Men* and *Twelve O'Clock High*, and role plays of typical leadership dilemmas to see how members responses reflect their understanding of program concepts. We also use games made up of short case descriptions coupled with multiple choice answers which provide group members with immediate feedback on their applications of leadership theory. Such methods help everyone to assess progress in understanding and applying new leadership techniques.

■ **Change in Related Systems**

Some groups have as their goal the education or change of other groups or organizations, (affirmative action programs, special interest lobby groups, social change groups, and community education groups). Other groups, such as college student executives or a Rotary Club, the Y, or scouts have a goal of providing leadership or community service to their related systems. These outside but related groups or systems can provide considerable feedback about the impact and effectiveness of the group under study. For example, a university's Centre for Innovative Student Activities received a wealth of information when they sent out a questionnaire asking about the impact of their activities to related students, faculty, and administration on campus.

Analyzing and Interpreting Information

In order to analyze your data, it is helpful to organize it into some kind of a framework or summary form from which hunches and interpretations can be made. If you are not sure where to start, the 'eyeballing' technique is most likely to be helpful.

The 'Eyeballing' Technique or Graphic Displays

A good place to start in summarizing and focusing your data is to display it graphically in a chart, diagram, graph, or listing of major points on flipchart sheets of paper. In preparing the sheets, we use different colours of marking pens to show categories of data.

Dimock's students have developed a group 'eyeballing' technique where they bring in the data from their human service activities on flipchart sheets, attach them to the wall and invite their classmates and Dimock to help analyze the information. As they look at the data they ask a lot of questions and look for relationships in what they see. First, they look for categories or classes: "does age or sex make a difference in enjoyment of the program?", "does length of participation in the program make a difference?", "does group size seem important?", and "are there any similarities among participants who think they learned the most?" Often, these exploratory questioning surveys lead to identifying some possible themes. These themes which are considered as possible 'rules of thumb' ask that students look for supporting evidence of the theme, (or negative evidence), elsewhere in the data. The next steps in data analysis, if any seem justified, become much clearer.

Numerical Scoring and Percentages

Much information can be put into categories on the basis of similarity in some respect and the results counted or tabulated. For example, the frequency with which members of a group perform different role functions can be determined using **Roles of Group Members,** (*How to Observe Your Group*, pp. 43–46). A numerical

FIGURE 22	Industrial Management Club (N=18)		
	1st Meeting	3rd Meeting	5th Meeting
Task Roles	81	74	68
Group Roles	12	16	24
Individual Roles	7	10	8

(Number of Roles of each Type per 100 Interactions)

scoring of the observations of the group observer showed the results seen in Figure 22.

An analysis of this information suggested that the group had been successful in increasing their group building roles, but the individual roles had stayed about the same.

Other typical areas that can be counted include attendance, number of program hours, frequency of verbal participation, number of products or projects completed, types of activities engaged in, phone calls or interactions between meetings, turnout for special events, turnover in the group showing seasonal fluctuations, differentiating males and females, age groups, length of membership, geographic location, and work group affiliation.

Information can also be put into categories that have some relationship to one another and scores assigned to the categories. In the example below of the **Survey of Group Development,** (*How to Observe Your Group*, pp. 41–43), scores were assigned to each of the four possible choices to each question reflecting a judgment of their desirability. A score of one was assigned to the answer seen as least desirable, and four to the most desirable. The degree of desirability is not exactly comparable for each question and a score of two is not twice as desirable as a score of one. The result is a rough overview that helps to show important trends and facilitates an analysis of the data.

Scoring is very popular as a data analysis method as it was such an important part of our school experience. Everything was given a score, (even gym), and when we asked "how did I do" we came to expect a score such as 27 out of 30 for an answer. Most of the nomination and sociometric techniques described here can be scored, as can many of the observation guides. While scores appear to be easily compared and contrasted, they tend to distort and oversimplify the data and hence are often most useful when coupled with a qualitative analysis method such as characteristic differences or ranking.

Content and Process Analysis

In qualitative analysis, the themes, nature, and characteristics of the data are explored to gain insights that may have been lost through rough scoring or tabulations. In **content analysis,** the descriptive data is divided into smaller parts or categories related to the goals of the group. Thus, the categories might be related to leadership styles, communication patterns, or factors contributing to group cohesion. The categories for analysis can also be created around perceived functional differences such as setting up major headings based on what group workers described in their daily log. Major headings or categories found in the logs were: descriptions of what the group did; comments on how the group liked the activity; reports of unique behaviour of individual members; and personal comments by the group worker.

Example

A sample of five out of thirty clubs of high school youth was selected and early in the program the worker of each completed a **Survey of Group Development,** (*How to Observe Your Group,* pp. 41–43). At the same time the professional staff who supervised the club program also completed a **Survey of Group Development** acting as an independent observer. Eight months later, the worker and supervisor again completed the survey independently. Scores of one to four were arbitrarily assigned the four categories for each question based on a judgment of their desirability (see Figure 23).

Process analysis looks at 'how the group worked' as contrasted to the 'what the group did' focus of content analysis. Usually, the two go hand in hand as the group's goal achievement is related to both effective group work and task accomplishment. In our Systems Improvement Research studies, we use a process-oriented method that describes the unfolding of a program as it moves forward, noting particularly critical events, collecting documents and experience reports, and systematically observing the impact of the program on the group members and other related systems.

Force Field Analysis

A **force field analysis** can be pictured as a giant tug-of-war with the factors contributing to something pulling in one direction and the restraining factors pulling in the opposite direction. A force field might ask "what are the forces contributing to the group's cohesion?", and "what are the forces detracting from it?" Or, more simply, it might be listing the factors strengthening the group's effectiveness and those weakening it.

An extension of the force field analysis is the **pro-con technique** where we make up a list of the successes and failures of

FIGURE 23

Club Scores Early and Late in Program Year

		Club A B* A*	Club B B A	Club C B A	Club D B A	Club E B A	Average B A
	1	3 - 3	3 - 4	2 - 3	3 - 3	2 - 4	2.6 - 3.4
	2	2 - 3	3 - 3	2 - 3	2 - 4	2 - 4	2.2 - 3.4
	3	2 - 4	2 - 3	2 - 4	2 - 3	1 - 3	1.9 - 3.4
	4	1 - 3	3 - 3	2 - 3	2 - 4	2 - 4	2.0 - 3.4
	5	1 - 3	3 - 4	1 - 2	3 - 3	3 - 4	2.2 - 3.2
Dimensions of Group Growth	6	2 - 2	2 - 3	2 - 4	3 - 4	2 - 3	2.2 - 3.2
	7	3 - 3	1 - 4	2 - 3	2 - 3	2 - 4	2.0 - 3.4
	8	2 - 3	2 - 2	3 - 4	2 - 4	2 - 3	2.2 - 3.2
	9	2 - 4	2 - 3	1 - 3	3 - 4	3 - 3	2.2 - 3.4
	10	1 - 3	3 - 3	2 - 4	4 - 4	2 - 4	2.2 - 3.6
	11	3 - 3	2 - 3	1 - 4	4 - 4	3 - 3	2.6 - 3.4
	12	3 - 4	3 - 3	2 - 3	3 - 4	3 - 3	2.8 - 3.4
	13	2 - 2	2 - 4	3 - 3	2 - 3	2 - 4	2.2 - 3.2
	Avg.	2.1 - 3.1	2.4 - 3.2	2.0 - 3.3	2.7 - 3.6	2.2 - 3.5	

*B = Before; A = After

our special events and then look for themes or characteristic differences between the two categories. This technique may also ask that we look at factors relating to a critical decision the group is about to make. In considering increasing the size of a group, relevant information could be divided into pros and cons to facilitate further analysis and aid in decision-making.

Characteristic Differences

After drawing up a force field analysis or two lists or groups of data in the pro-con technique, it is possible to start 'eyeballing' the two lists looking for factors which are characteristic of list A, but not of group B, and vice versa. These factors do not have to be true for every item on the list, but are generally characteristic of that group as a whole and in ways that are different from the other group. After you have noted the characteristic differences for each group, look them over and see if there are any generalizing principles which account for the differences between the two lists. For example, in looking at two lists of factors associated with high and low days of patient attacks (abuse) of the health care staff, it was noted that low risk periods were associated with:

1. Full complement of on duty staff.
2. Structured activity involving most patients had taken place during the previous seven hours.
3. Recent snacks or meals had not included any high energy foods (chocolate) or excessive stimulants (coke, coffee).
4. An activity or event on which the patients could focus was to occur within the next 24 hours.
5. The staff had made rounds visiting all patients for brief interactions, (they had been highly visible).
6. The staff team included at least one male member.

As an evaluation method, several people will look over the two lists or groups of data and seek out the characteristic differences. If the goal is to help make decisions or improve program planning, the people looking at the lists will likely be key people involved in the decision-making process, or staff involved in program planning. However, if the goal is to establish an unbiased evaluation, then outside **judges** will be used to establish the characteristic differences or rank the items. These judges, (three to five usually), should not know anything more than necessary about the evaluation project and should be presented with the two lists or group of data and asked to find as many characteristic differences as possible between the two lists. Ideally, the judges should be people who are knowledgeable in the field and familiar with the criteria they are being asked to use in judging the lists.

The essence of the method of characteristic differences is to create two groups which will differ in some way and compare the data. The two groups can be created in many different ways: males vs. females; classroom A vs. classroom B; rapidly healing patients vs. slow healing; successful programs vs. unsuccessful; long-term participants vs. short-term; high achievers vs. low; youth whose parents participate in the program vs. those who don't; and top half vs. bottom half.

This method can be used with all the various data collection procedures described here, but it is particularly useful with descriptive data such as that collected by P.M.R.'s, journals, descriptive program records, anecdotal records, thumbnail descriptions, process observations, and self-reports or descriptions. It can, however, also be used with peer ratings, sociometric measurements, reputation ratings, community and organizational assessments, (indicators of the quality of life), and needs assessments. It is the most useful method for analyzing the characteristics of successful and unsuccessful programs, and helping groups to build on the strengths in their program.

Ranking

Ranking is the process of arranging a set of data from high to low, according to some criterion. We are thinking in ranks when we ascertain the status hierarchy in our group, put members in a continuum according to their contribution to task accomplishment, or make up a list of member interests from most important to least important. Using a method of ranking, a great deal of qualitative or description information can be put into comparative order more easily and analyzed more fully than putting it into specific categories, which may be artificial and not promote establishing relationships. And, if it becomes important to establish more reliable relationships, rank order correlations are the most time effective.[5]

Reflecting on Group Theory

We have presented a considerable amount of group theory in *Making Workgroups Effective* and *How to Observe Your Group*. A theory is a summary of numerous actual experiences and gives some focus or perspective to these experiences. These theories can provide very useful frameworks for analyzing group data. For example, the use of the **Group Observation Guide,** (*How to Observe Your Group*, p. 36), or a sociometric measurement can be explored using the Interpersonal Relations Theory of Group Development and hunching, where the group is at this time in handling the developmental tasks of inclusion, control, and openness. Pro and con categories, or strengths and weaknesses, could be established for each task as an aid to analyzing and interpreting the information. Likewise, the factors contributing to strong, productive groups, (*Making Workgroups Effective*, p. 27 ff; and *Managing Dynamic Groups*, p. 1 ff), can also be used as a framework or provide categories for analyzing group or individual data.

Reporting Back to Your Group

Before you plan a report or make up a diagnostic analysis to present to the group, let us remind you of the principle that involvement in a group's analysis and diagnosing of a group's strengths and weaknesses is a more powerful motivator than receiving crisp, well presented conclusions or a credible, well-documented report. Thus, we suggest that before you consider carrying the ball through the data analysis phase, you consider ways of involving the group in analyzing and interpreting the data. In addition to increasing their interest in revitalizing their group, you'll gain their experience in

---

5   Ranking procedures and rank order correlations are described in H.G. Dimock, *Simplified Guide to Program Evaluation*, pp. 53–58.

the group to give additional perspective in analyzing the data. The group owns the data and they are empowered to make whatever use of it they choose. Data analysis and interpretation are usually best done as a group activity to optimize the group building potential, and some kind of graphic or pictorial summary is helpful to work from as well as digests of the raw data. It may be productive to set aside a special meeting or at least part of a regular one for this group activity.

Another rule of thumb is to arrange these data analyses and interpretive sessions as soon after the data is collected as is practical. This was a major finding in our Systems Improvement Research studies and led us to target the next meeting for feedback and analysis of data collected. Over a period of time we have found it very worthwhile to set up rotating teams of group members, (usually three), to organize the data collection and analysis activity, with the total group participating under their direction. We hope these ideas have given you information you can use to make your group more effective, and that you have some fun with your group in implementing them.

PART THREE

Understanding Work Groups and Their Environment

Up to this point in the book, we've discussed ways to understand groups by focusing on behaviours that build, strengthen, and regulate group life and solve the groups' objective tasks. For many years, groups have been discussed as if they were isolated entities whose operations were unaffected by larger systems, but nothing can be farther from the truth. Groups are almost always parts of larger systems. While members of a group take care of routine business and plan for its future, events occur within the group's environment that also require attention. Most groups function within the boundaries of organizations and institutions. Groups don't usually work in isolation and are generally part of an external environment, e.g. an agency, a company, a department, or the group's context when we want to assess its development and productivity. The ability of a group to function is achieved when there is a balance between the processes of influence within it and the environment in which it functions.

Some of the interacting pieces in a group's environment might include field offices, central offices, laws, new technologies, outdated technologies, stockholders, and the corporate image. In trying to understand the functioning of a group and its internal dynamics, it's important to have a clear picture of the interacting layers within an organization that seem to have an effect on the internal dynamics of the group. The external happenings may be deliberate or unintentional, but they need to be understood and internal responses are required.

Rather than sitting on the group boundary and only looking inward, we also have to take into account the behaviours directed outward, toward other parts of the organization. That is, we have to take an external perspective to understand internal group process and performance. Group members interact with one another but they are also proactive with outsiders; they seek information and resources; they communicate with other units; and lobby for scarce resources; e.g. clients, funding. So, we must ask how the organization influences the group, and how the group reaches out to its environment when we try to assess a group.

Studies indicate that when work groups — or teams, as they are commonly called — rated their own performance, groups felt they performed well when they concentrated their efforts internally and they didn't rate their performance as high when they had frequent external interactions. Previous research studies suggest that external activities interfere with the development of effective internal operations, but internal cohesion can promote external stereotyping and may eliminate important external information needed to perform effectively.

Groups may be underbounded — having many external ties but an inability to coalesce and motivate members to pull together their external knowledge — or overbounded — having high internal loyalty but an inability to reach out to its external environment. We need to know what forces are operating on the group at that time. Demand for a product or program influences the public image of the group and as this image increases or decreases, it may affect the way the group works and regulates its program or product.

Work Group Effectiveness

Work groups or teams need the ability to quickly and efficiently adapt to current conditions. To do so, members need access to objective information about areas that need improvement and about areas in which they excel. Team assessments is one strategy that assists members in collecting information about how the group is functioning as a work unit.

There are a number of standardized surveys designed to provide feedback to teams about elements that are important to effective team functioning. These types of surveys are useful in identifying team strengths and weaknesses and in stimulating discussions about critical team performance issues. They also assist in focusing action-planning to help improve team effectiveness and in providing feedback about how the team is meeting both internal and external needs.

Many surveys measure a variety of items including availability of information, performing successfully, adequate support from the organization, clear vision and goals, and the value team members feel for their contributions.

Surveys can also be developed to include items that are of particular relevance to the work group. Below is a list of items that could be included in a short survey developed for a specific purpose:

- mission clarity.
- team unity.
- role clarity.
- empowerment.
- trust and support.
- skills.
- commitment.
- innovation.

- satisfaction.
- performance.
- leadership.
- information.
- material resources.
- rewards.
- organizational support.
- team coordination.

The survey is completed by team members and can also be given to others outside the team such as co-workers, suppliers, and clients. Each team member indicates how effectively he/she thinks the team is performing; the others provide a second source of feedback on how effective they believe the team's performance is in relation to the objectives of the larger environment.

These types of surveys assist teams in assessing team strengths and weaknesses and can be used to identify actions to help improve team effectiveness. When used in an ongoing manner, they can be viewed as continuous improvement initiatives in that they benchmark team effectiveness and provide critical feedback for future modification and action.

Figure 24 shows a sample of a few items and corresponding scales as one example of how to compile a survey to meet the assessment needs of a team.

Analysis of Inter-group Dynamics

Inter-group dynamics refers to relationships between groups or departments, within a system or organization.

The effectiveness of any group is dependent on the relations between different groups in the environment. Groups, like individuals, make social comparisons with one another and make control demands on one another. Members of one group often have active contacts with members of another body. Top executives meet with their board members, union representatives confer with management and the public relations unit needs information from program units. Such interactions across the boundaries of groups can develop in unexpected ways, and often they are marked by tension because it isn't always clear what rules should be followed. These ambiguities may lead to strong responses, and groups' connections may be burdened with conflict and hard feelings.

On the positive side, inter-group conflict and rivalries can result in increased motivation through competition and can also increase the cohesion within each group. However, when competition escalates into destructive conflict, 'winning' becomes more important than reaching organizational goals.

FIGURE 24   *Board, Team, or Committee Survey*

PURPOSE: (Clarity and agreement of purpose and priorities).

What do you think are the goals of this board/coordinating committee?

1. _____

2. _____

3. _____

How clear are these goals to you? ☐ not clear ☐ fuzzy ☐ clear
How clear are they to others? ☐ not clear ☐ fuzzy ☐ clear
What are your top 3 action priorities for the next three months?

1. _____

2. _____

3. _____

ROLES: (Clarity and agreement of roles and responsibilities).

How clear are you about your role and responsibility on this board/committee?
       ☐ not clear ☐ fuzzy ☐ clear
How clear are other members about their roles and responsibilities?
       ☐ not clear ☐ fuzzy ☐ clear

PROCEDURES: (Clarity about how the group will work).

How clear are procedures for making decisions?
       ☐ not clear ☐ fuzzy ☐ clear
How clear are procedures for solving problems?
       ☐ not clear ☐ fuzzy ☐ clear
How clear are procedures for setting priorities?
       ☐ not clear ☐ fuzzy ☐ clear

INTERPERSONAL: (Degree of trust, support, and respect).

How much do members trust one another?
       ☐ little ☐ some ☐ a lot
How much do members support one another?
       ☐ little ☐ some ☐ a lot
How much do members respect one another?
       ☐ little ☐ some ☐ a lot

Understanding both discordant relations and pleasant alliances between groups is an important ingredient in group success.

Some important areas to monitor in inter-group contexts include the following:

- responsibility for tasks.
- procedures for completing tasks.
- contacts between groups.
- resources of groups.
- size of groups.
- loyalty to the group.
- evaluation of own group.
- solutions proposed by each group.
- importance of issues.
- members' dispositions.
- cultural conditioning.
- authority's role in restraining hostile behaviour.

Organizational Scans:
Frameworks for Assessing Work Group Context

There are many different types of surveys and frameworks that can be used to collect information about the context in which a group operates. The information can then be used to help a group modify its dynamics and plan future strategies to assist the group in operating effectively and achieving its longer term goals.

Figure 25 presents an organization scan that we designed for use in Human Service Organizations to help them assess the changing realities of the not-for-profit sector. It has a specific focus on the areas of operation that have been the most subject to change in the past few years, and the ones most likely to change in the next few years. By thinking of this sample scan as a tool, we can conduct analyses in a purposeful manner by using a systematic process. The information collected can be used to identify opportunities or constraints for the group so a plan of action to achieve the group's long term objectives can be implemented. The categories listed below can be used as needed for a particular assessment. Figure 24 (showing a Board survey) may be a good place to start if the Board is going to give leadership to a process of conducting a broader organization scan, analyzing it, and planning for the application of any new insights it provides. Two areas to investigate are the internal environment of the organization — of which the group is a part — and the organization's external environment, (see Figure 26).

1. What three activities, in your view, have the highest prestige here?

   A.

   B.

   C.

   Now go back and indicate the extent these activities reflect the stated organization goals (high – medium – low)

2. List the four major groups of clients served in this organization and rate their likely evaluation of your work. Likely rating (high – medium – low)

   A.

   B.

   C.

   D.

   How clearly identified are your targeted groups of clients?

   What percentage of your possible group of clients know about your program?

   What do your clients most value of what you do?

3. How do you get information about how effective your programs are? How reliable and useful is this data?

4. Rate the effectiveness of your programs.

   1 (Low) ———— 2 ———— 3 (Med.) ———— 4 ———— 5 (High)

5. Rate the effectiveness of the volunteer program, (recruitment, placement, orientation, training, and recognition).

   1 (Low) ———— 2 ———— 3 (Med.) ———— 4 ———— 5 (High)

6. Rate the effectiveness of the management of your finances.

   1 (Low) ———— 2 ———— 3 (Med.) ———— 4 ———— 5 (High)

7. Rate the effectiveness of your fundraising.

   1 (Low) ——— 2 ——— 3 (Med.) ——— 4 ——— 5 (High)

8. At your Board, (or National Board), level, rate the following (1 to 5; with 1 as Low and 5 as High):

   Rating

   A. Clarity of agreement of purposes and priorities. _____
   B. Clarity of agreement of roles and responsibilities. _____
   C. Clarity and effectiveness about procedures for setting priorities, making decisions, and solving problems. _____
   D. Degree of trust, support, and respect among Board members. _____

9. How is the organization positioned in the external community, (business, media, political), to maintain its status and its clear identity of providing for the special needs of your client group?

   What percentage of time and energy goes into networking and building relationships with other organizations that share similar goals? How much payoff is there from it?

10. What is the effect on this organization of present changing social, economic, and demographic conditions? Changes in health services, diagnostic and treatment advances, new technologies and discoveries? Changes in the educational system? Shifts in moral and cultural values and ways of doing things? Communication technology advances in computers, information highway, direct satellite TV, etc.

   What is affecting us the most?

   Where are the new opportunities?

   Where are the new threats?

11. What is the effect, if any, on this organization of recent government actions such as: reductions or shifts in funding; setting new funding priorities; increasing control

...continued

over your operation by reviews, additional regulations, licences or permits, investigations, audits, program evaluations, charitable status review, certification requirements, changes in taxes or tax status, insurance requirements, affirmative action, employment equity, workers' compensation and other legal regulations; shifts in service delivery regulations such as Health System Renewals and Integrated Service Centres?

What is having an impact on you?

Where are there new opportunities with these changes?

Where are there new threats with these changes?

FIGURE 26   *Environment Scan*

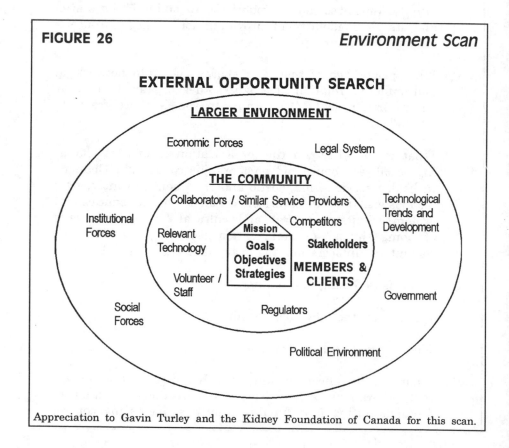

Appreciation to Gavin Turley and the Kidney Foundation of Canada for this scan.

62

Internal Organization Catagories

■ Board of Directors (experience, skills, commitment)

■ Top Management (experience, skills, management style)
  • how does Board and top management get data on organization's strengths and weaknesses, if at all?
  • how to they get external data to assess the organization's threats and opportunities?

■ Organization values, mission, goals and objectives, and strategies

■ Critical structures needed to support the organization (funding, budgeting, communication and promotion, human resource development, programs, products, or services, etc.)

External Organization Catagories

■ Sector of Operation Activity
  • what is happening and what is about to happen in the sector in which the organization operates?

■ Competitors

■ Customers and other stakeholders

■ Government Regulations

■ Labour Unions and other pressure groups

■ Demographics

■ Economy

■ Technology

Conclusion

People working with groups have found the scene is rapidly changing, while what groups are doing and how they are doing it adjusts to the new economic, social, and demographic realities. The baby boomers are in their 50s! In this process, the level or responsibility and accountability has increased. More and more "the powers that be" are expecting to see measurable performance outcomes — hard data — about the groups they manage or finance. This book has described the most practical ways to provide credible reports of a group's measurable indicators of success. In the assessment process, group leaders and members alike will have explored new perspectives on their group which they can use to build group strength and personal satisfaction.

63

Bibliography

Bettenhausen, K.L. "Five years of group research: what we have learned and what needs to be addressed." *Journal of Management*, 17: 345–81, 1991.

Brewer, M.B. and R.M. Kramer. "The Psychology of Intergroup Attitudes and Behaviour", *Annual Review of Psychology*, 36: 219–43, 1985.

Brown, L.D. *Managing Conflict at Organizational Interfaces*. Reading, MA: Addison-Wesley, 1983.

Dimock, H.G. *How to Observe Your Group*, 3rd ed. North York, ON: Captus Press, 1993.

——. *Intervention and Empowerment: Helping Organizations to Change*. North York, ON: Captus Press, 1992.

——. *A Simplified Guide to Program Evaluation*. North York, ON: Captus Press, 1987.

Dimock, H.G. and I. Devine. *Managing Dynamic Groups*, 3rd ed. North York, ON: Captus Press, 1996.

——. *Making Workgroups Effective*, 3rd ed. North York, ON: Captus Press, 1994.

Judd, C.M., E.R. Smith, and L.H. Kidder. *Research Methods in Social Relations*, 6th ed. New York: Holt, Rinehart and Winston, 1991.

Likert, R. *The Human Organization: Its Management and Value*. New York: McGraw-Hill, 1967.

Patton, M.Q. *Qualitative Evaluation and Research Methods*, 2nd ed. Newbury Park, CA: Sage Publications, 1990.

Wheelan, S. *Group Processes: A Developmental Perspective*. Toronto, ON: Allyn and Bacon, 1994.

Zander, A. *Making Workgroups Effective*. San Francisco: Jossey-Bass, 1983.